CASPER HAUSER

Borgo Press Books by AUGUSTE ANICET-BOURGEOIS

Casper Hauser (with Adolphe d'Ennery)
The Hunchback (with Paul Féval)
Macbeth (with Victor Ducange)
The Venetian (with Alexandre Dumas)

Borgo Press Books by ADOLPHE D'ENNERY

Casper Hauser (with Auguste Anicet-Bourgeois)
The Children of Captain Grant (with Jules Verne)
Faust
Michael Strogoff (with Jules Verne)
The Story of a Flag
The Voyage Through the Impossible (with Jules Verne)

CASPER HAUSER

A PLAY IN FOUR ACTS

AUGUSTE ANICET-BOURGEOIS &

ADOLPHE D'ENNERY

Translated and Adapted by Frank J. Morlock

THE BORGO PRESS
MMXIII

CASPER HAUSER

Copyright © 2006, 2007, 2013 by Frank J. Morlock

FIRST BORGO PRESS EDITION

Published by Wildside Press LLC

www.wildsidebooks.com

DEDICATION

To the memory of my instructor and friend,
Joseph Borozne

CONTENTS

CAST OF CHARACTERS 9
PREFACE 11
ACT I 13
ACT II 49
ACT III 75
ACT IV 119
ABOUT THE TRANSLATOR 151

CAST OF CHARACTERS

CASPER HAUSER

SCHWARTZ

THE COUNT

FREDERIC

FRITZ

KLAUS

AN AULIC COUNCILOR

A PEASANT

A VALET

THE BARONESS

MINA

SAIA, a beggar girl

A PEASANT GIRL

Aulic Councilors, Masons, Peasants, Valets

PREFACE

All Germany, then later, the whole of Europe, echoed with the misfortunes and cruel captivity of Casper Hauser.

Torn from his mother's arms at birth, he was thrown into a cell where eighteen years of his life unfolded. There, deprived of light and sunshine, having only some shreds of clothes to cover himself with, and to appease his hunger only a little bread which his guardian from time to time threw him—he endured unheard of tortures during this long space of time.

And later, when freed by a miracle, it seemed a happier life was promised him. When already, his promptly developed intelligence made him experience the harms of life, caused him to admire the marvels of creation, to which, he, poor prisoner was to live a stranger, his persecutors reawakened more numerous and more relentless.

Several times they attempted his life. In vain the Court of Vienna tried to protect him; his enemies, who, surrounded by a deep mystery, knew how to approach him without cease, for they were high and mighty; for if the secret of the birth of their victim had been discovered, a great name would have been substituted for that of Casper Hauser.

The poor child was obliged to succumb in this unequal struggle, and Casper Hauser died, carrying with him into the tomb the names of his cruel persecutors, and the secret of his birth.

The drama that Casper Hauser inspired was written, rehearsed, and played in nineteen days. That says enough of all the gratitude the authors owe to the artists who seconded them with their talent and their zeal, to the skilled painters who improvised the delightful decorations of the Second Act; finally, to the directors, who, taking the reins of administration, have completely demonstrated tireless activity.

—Auguste Anicet-Bourgeois & Adolphe d'Ennery
June 6, 1838

ACT I

The Action takes place in 1823. The stage represents a low hall in old castle of Ranspach in Austria. On one side, a stairway leading to a cellar used as a sepulcher by the Masters of Ranspach. On the other side, a grand and large staircase leading to apartments. At the back, a door leading to the terrace of the Park.

AT RISE, it is night.

FRITZ

(alone)

This devil of a Frantz doesn't get here. He really was sent far. Because he found Mr. Frederick, our young doctor! He's the only one that the Baroness is willing to receive, and she must be very ill, that poor lady, because the old Count, her father, who ordinarily shows himself so harsh, so cruel to her—to rush all terrified to demand a doctor. It's quite late—it's singular, but at night I don't like to find myself alone in this old tower and near this door. That's where the ancestors of the Count repose, and if a few of them, while alive, had been of the humor of their offshoot, he has nothing good to expect from them after his death— What weather! What a storm!

(a gust of wind opens the window)

Huh? What's that?

(the light goes out)

Come on, right—no more light. Happily, here's an armchair. I can go to sleep while waiting—because I know myself—I'm capable of being afraid— Ah, ah! I think that I am getting drowsy. Yes, now that's what: I am getting sleepy. Now, who's that coming—good night, my friend Fritz—g'night.

(he falls asleep)

SCHWARTZ

(wrapped in a cloak, coming furtively down the stairs)

Why do I always tremble when approaching this terrible cellar? Why does my soul revolt when I come to accomplish this duty I imposed on myself? Eighteen years do not suffice to stifle conscience—remorse never ceases to awake! And yet, to recall my courage and put my memory to sleep, I've had, as usual, recourse to drunkenness—but my thoughts are more powerful than the wine.

(turning his lamp toward a table at one side)

It ought to be placed here again.

(pours himself a drink and drinks)

It's only in his presence that I tremble. I actually weep. Dawn will soon come; let's get a move on.

(he heads toward the cellar, and bumps into Fritz's armchair. Fritz lets out a yell.)

SCHWARTZ

(whose mind is distracted)

Who are you? How'd you get in? Go back to the cellar, wretch.

FRITZ

(aside)

It's Schwartz.

SCHWARTZ

Get back in there, I tell you! You don't know what's going on with your life. If you haven't been killed in eighteen years, you'll be killed today.

FRITZ

Who says they're going to kill me? Why it's me, it's me, Mr. Schwartz.

SCHWARTZ

(coming to)

That voice—

FRITZ

It's the voice of Fritz, who has no desire to go in where you say—

SCHWARTZ

Fritz—did I speak? What did I say? Answer, answer!

FRITZ

Hell, Mr. Schwartz—you—you asked me why I was here.

SCHWARTZ

Indeed—what are you doing here? Such an hour? Go away.

FRITZ

No way— I'm ordered to stay.

SCHWARTZ

And as for me, I'm ordering you to leave.

FRITZ

But it's by the Count, my master.

SCHWARTZ

I am master, too, I am.

(seizing Fritz by the arm)

And I know how to make myself obeyed.

FRITZ

I'm obeying, I'm obeying, Mr. Schwartz.

SCHWARTZ

Get out, I want to be alone.

(Mina enters with a candle.)

MINA

Oh, my God! What's going on?

SCHWARTZ

(to Fritz)

Shut up!

(aloud)

Nothing, nothing, Miss Mina.— How is it you are still up at this hour?

MINA

Are you the only one in the Château who's unaware of the condition of my poor godmother?

SCHWARTZ

The Baroness?

MINA

She's very ill tonight. The Count has sent for my cousin Frederick, the doctor, and I came to find out if he's got here.

FRITZ

No, Miss, no.

SCHWARTZ

(aside)

Poor woman!

MINA

Then I'm going to wait here. I want to speak to him before he goes up.

SCHWARTZ

(aside)

What a contretemps! How to go in now? It's impossible during the day—

There are people around here constantly.

MINA

Mr. Fritz—is there no one here who might go to meet my cousin and hurry his arrival?

FRITZ

Yes, miss.

SCHWARTZ

I myself will go.

MINA

I didn't dare ask it of you.

SCHWARTZ

Why? I, too, love the Baroness.

MINA

Hasten then, Mr. Schwartz.

SCHWARTZ

(eyeing the cellar door as he leaves)

Come—until the next night.

(Schwartz leaves)

FRITZ

In the condition he's in, and with this weather, he's capable of falling dead drunk on the road.

MINA

How is it that the Count who is so strict can keep such a man?

FRITZ

That's what everyone asks and no one can understand.

MINA

He's always dismal and coarse.

FRITZ

Coarse in words and gestures.

MINA

Spending most of his life strolling alone in the park.

FRITZ

And spending the rest of his time getting drunk in his room. Well, it's all the same. The Count is indulgent only to him—he won't endure his leaving the château.

MINA

Oh, maybe there's some great secret between these two men.

FRITZ

I had that idea at first. In the distractions that always accompany his intoxication, Schwartz speaks of the Count, of old man Schwartz, and then, I don't know, of someone he always refers to simply as "him".

MINA

And then he denies all authority, he defies orders given to him, and only the appearance of the Count calms him.

FRITZ

And, just now, actually, I heard him saying things—

MINA

What?

FRITZ

Things that I will only speak of to the Count.

(aside)

If I have my share of the secret, I'll also have my share of the favor.

COUNT

(entering)

Well, how do you feel?

BARONESS

It seems to me that after this terrible crisis, the air of

the park would do me good—but I trusted my strength too much. I can hardly support myself.

COUNT

A chair—quick—a chair!

FRITZ

Here.

MINA

My poor godmother.

BARONESS

It's you, child? Frederic is awfully slow.

COUNT

Even this morning you were less ill. What cause has brought on such a great change tonight?

BARONESS

What cause? It's that the night which is unfolding is the 10th of June—father—it's that this night I was just eighteen.

COUNT

Silence! Let everyone leave, and let no one come in until the doctor arrives—

(all leave)

COUNT

(striding up and down)

Are you pleased, then, Madame, to confide to all these strangers our family secrets? Does it please you to make me blush before my valets?

BARONESS

Perhaps you are right. My soul, weakened by sorrows and tears, no longer knows how to keep a secret. Well, instead of a doctor, have a priest called, father—give me the right to die, and you will be safe in the honor of your name.

COUNT

Die! Always that word! That's not the way people die, Madame. The sorrows of the soul are slow at sapping life. They torture and don't kill. I've actually suffered, too, for the last eighteen years. I've seen my name ready to be blasted, my family coat of arms ready to be dragged in the mud— Oh, yes, I have really suffered— as much as you, more than you, perhaps—because I'm a man, and I don't have, as you do, tears which wash away sorrow.

BARONESS

You speak of your sorrows, sir, and what of me, poor woman, what has my life been? Not just for the last eighteen years—but since I was born? When I lost my mother, I was still quite young—but not young enough so that this loss didn't tear my soul apart. And then—overwhelmed by the weight of this first blow, I sought around me a tender affection which sustained my courage and helped me to live—when my tearful eyes sought a friend, they only met the proud and icy glance of my father. And when later, in default of your heart, another—who understood me—filled with devotion, and love—when this poor Leone—

COUNT

Enough! Never utter that infamous name—who, abusing the hospitality I'd given him, wasn't afraid to dishonor my only child.

BARONESS

(forcefully and standing straight up)

He's dead, sir—and God alone has the right to judge him.

(She collapses, overwhelmed)

COUNT

He brought shame and dishonor into my family, and I wasn't even able to avenge myself.

BARONESS

Don't weep over your lost vengeance, for in default of a spouse, a child remains to you—and the mother—and you haven't spared them. Deaf to my cries, without pity for my tears, you took my child. And as for me, crazy, I repeated endlessly, "Give him back to me." They took him from me to hide him from all eyes—but he'll be returned to me, because one doesn't kill a poor child, one doesn't strangle it without pity. Let them take my life, mine, his mother. I alone am guilty, perhaps that's just—but him, my son, my child—he exists and I will see him soon.

COUNT

You are still mistaken.

BARONESS

Yes, by joining perfidy to cruelty, you profited by my mistake. You said: "Accept the spouse I've chosen for you, and your child will live"; and as for me, I deceived that man, I did an infamous thing to save my son, and after this odious marriage, when I asked to see him—for a moment, for a single moment—you said to me, "I had him killed."

COUNT

It was necessary that the honor of my family not be soiled. The tomb is discreet.

(enter Mina, Servants, Fritz)

MINA

Here he is, here he is, Madame.

COUNT

Who is it?

MINA

Frederic—my cousin, the doctor that you had called.

COUNT

Let him come, then.

FREDERIC

(entering)

Pardon me, Madame, and you, Milord Count, if I made you wait. But when you sent to the Presbytery I'd just left, and it's only by chance that I learned of the new crisis which has struck Madame.

(he approaches the Baroness and takes her hand)

Still quite a violent agitation.

BARONESS

No—I am less ill.

FREDERIC

Poor woman. Milord Count, the one who made me rush here is one of your men, by name of Schwartz, that I met on the way in terrible disorder. I was hardly able to grasp that my presence was desired here; the man's reason seemed lost.

COUNT

What are you saying? Schwartz, the wretch. Ah, he's drunk again.

FREDERIC

Milord Count, intoxication doesn't result in ideas of death and blood like this—he was in a delirium of remorse.

FRITZ

What's more—

COUNT

Who dares to speak?

FRITZ

Pardon, Milord Count—but I was saying, moreover, this evening, near the cellar, I witnessed things that—

COUNT

What happened?

FRITZ

(mysteriously)

Imagine, Milord Count, that he, thinking himself alone, said words—

COUNT

(interrupting him)

That you will repeat only in front of me. Come.

(to valets)

Run on the highway and bring the wretch back here. Doctor Frederic, I'm leaving you with my daughter; don't leave her during the night.

FREDERIC

I promise you that, sir.

(the Count leaves, Fritz follows him.)

FRITZ

Now here's my moment of favor or my ruin. I'm atrociously frightened.

(he leaves)

BARONESS

Now that we are at last alone, my friends, I can breathe easily, without curious looks trying to spy out my thoughts—and without an iron will weighing on my soul.

MINA

Oh—affection, tenderness, that's what you will get from us.

FREDERIC

Madame—it's not only as a friend, but as a doctor that you had me called.

BARONESS

Don't speak to me of your art—it is powerless against the illness that consumes me. In my home, you see—it's the soul which is killing my body and I've hastened to end it—or indeed, if I still ask for a few years to live—it will be to bless your marriage with Mina, for you love each other, you are worthy of each other, and no one will come to snatch her from your arms.

FREDERIC

Who knows—poor doctor, without fortune—without fame.

BARONESS

A name? You will know how to aggrandize yours; a fortune? But I have no friends but the two of you, and I will die soon.

MINA

Madame—

BARONESS

I will die when your marriage is accomplished—yes, you will be his wife. And if heaven grants you a child, oh, be careful of it, poor mother—keep it at your breast, and let no one tear it from you! You can hug your child—oh, how happy you will be. Yes, you can hug your child.

MINA

What's she mean?

FREDERIC

(low)

Don't you know that heaven has refused her the consolation of being a mother?

(to Baroness)

Madame, thoughts like these are killing you, and I mustn't allow—

BARONESS

Let me be, let me be, my friend. I want to think of the happiness of those I love.

FREDERIC

See, you are more pale again, your hand's trembling, and the damp cold of the room can be fatal to you. Go back to your room, Madame.

BARONESS

No!

(a great uproar is heard)

What's that disturbance?

FRITZ

(looking)

They're bringing back Schwartz.

BARONESS

Schwartz! The sight of that man makes me ill! You are right, my friends, it might be better to go back to my room. He's coming in this direction. Oh, give me support so that I don't meet him.

(They climb the stairway and disappear.)

SCHWARTZ

(intoxicated, entering with several valets)

Why are you dragging me here? I don't want to stay here, I want to leave.

(the valets bar his passage.)

Why are you forcing me to dwell in this château whose walls weigh on me like a sepulcher! Indeed, you see that it's killing me—that I cannot do it! But, I don't want to stay here! Night! Night! Night! I will come here by myself, without being seen— I will come for him.

(the valets look at each other in astonishment)

But now, I want to leave!

(forcefully)

Do you hear? I want to leave!

Make way for me, or I'll beat a way open for myself by force.

(they push him back)

Get back then— I intend to be obeyed.

COUNT

(appearing at the top of the stairs)

Who dares raise his voice here? Who permits himself to give orders in my château?

(coming down)

So it's you—speak!

SCHWARTZ

(removing his hat and bowing)

Me—no, no, Milord Count.

COUNT

There's only one master here, and only one will. I'm that master—that will is mine.

Whoever resists, I kick him out.

(to Schwartz)

Or I will punish him even more severely.

SCHWARTZ

(humbly)

Yes, master, you are strict, but you are just. And you are not the one who forbids your poor Schwartz to stroll in the avenues of the château.

COUNT

One strolls in the daytime. At night, one sleeps.

SCHWARTZ

(low)

But there are those who no longer sleep—

COUNT

(low)

For those I have other orders.

(to Valets)

Leave us now.

(the valets leave)

SCHWARTZ

(low and sobering up little by little)

Other orders, he says.

COUNT

Those who no longer sleep have remorse in their soul—and when courage fails them like weak women, when they no longer have strength to struggle against remorse, they get drunk and reveal profound mysteries.

SCHWARTZ

Milord, I've said nothing. I've said nothing.

COUNT

Those—they separate them.

SCHWARTZ

Separate from me?

COUNT

You will leave today; you will go await me at my Château Risburg.

SCHWARTZ

Leave! Leave! Oh, no, no—that's impossible—you cannot exact that.

COUNT

I wish it!

SCHWARTZ

(aside)

But him, him—what will become of him?

COUNT

(aside)

He refuses. Fritz told the truth.

(aloud)

I am going to give orders that you will be separated as

of this very night.

SCHWARTZ

This night! Oh, no, no, Milord. If it's drunkenness you worry about, well! I swear to you to master myself. But in the name of heaven, Milord.

(looking at the cellar)

Oh—don't send me away! Don't send me away!

COUNT

(aside)

No more doubt, and that talk—that would kill you today.

(calling)

Fritz! Fritz!

FRITZ

Milord called me?

SCHWARTZ

(aside)

What's he going to do?

FRITZ

(aside)

Now favor is going to begin.

COUNT

You are going to have horses harnessed to my post-chaise.

FRITZ

Yes, Milord—and then?

COUNT

And then—

FRITZ

(aside)

Let's see the favor coming.

COUNT

You will yourself escort Schwartz to my Château at Risburg.

SCHWARTZ

But—

COUNT

Silence!

FRITZ

And after that?

COUNT

You'll bring the chaise back, that's all.

FRITZ

(aside)

That's all—well, and the favor—what about it?

COUNT

Go and hurry up.

(Fritz starts to leave)

Ah—listen?

FRITZ

(aside)

I knew he was going to call me back. There it is—this little favor.

COUNT

Make Herman the Mason come right away.

SCHWARTZ

A Mason? And why, why? Mercy.

COUNT

An ancient custom has it that the door of this cellar, sepulcher of my ancestors, is to remain walled up until a member of my family has descended there. I've failed in this custom. It's an omission I intend to repair immediately.

(he gestures to Fritz who moves away)

FRITZ

(leaving)

Up to now my share in the secret is not a good thing.

(he leaves)

SCHWARTZ

Come on—I've got to tell him everything.

COUNT

Well—don't you have any preparations to make? I really intend that you leave.

SCHWARTZ

So be it! I will leave if you still insist on it, but before I go I must object to the accomplishment of the last order you just gave. Milord, the door to this cellar must not be walled up.

COUNT

You would dare?

SCHWARTZ

You know indeed that I always obey you slavishly— You know that on your part, a sign, a glance suffices for me and I bow my head. But this time, I repeat, your order cannot be carried out.

COUNT

Who will prevent it?

SCHWARTZ

You, Milord Count, when I've revealed a humble secret to you.

COUNT

I'm listening.

SCHWARTZ

One night eighteen years ago, when I was already in your service—you came to me pale, clothes in disorder carrying a child whose cries you stifled; then placing it in my arms you said, "Take it!" and when I asked what I ought to do with it, "Kill it!" Such was your response.

COUNT

I said it.

SCHWARTZ

Because I wasn't a murderer, I refused to bathe my hands in the blood of an infant—whatever the price you were willing to pay for the crime. But it wasn't gold that you brought to constrain me. No, you had in your hands a means a thousand times more powerful—you disposed of the life of my father, and placing before my eyes a fatal paper: "Read!" you told me. "Your father or this child." Oh, if you had asked me for my life, if I'd been able to choose between my death and that of the victim, I wouldn't have hesitated, I would have killed myself in front of you; but I had to save the life of my father, and when bearing the child away, I was going to leave your park, when a man suddenly presented himself before me—shocked, fearing being discovered, I hid the child under my cloak. The man kept coming closer, and the child started crying—all was lost. A small cellar was nearby. I threw the victim in, and striding toward the one who was coming, I forced him to turn back on his steps, for fear that the cries I already heard had reached him. These cries that are tearing my soul apart, and that you also, Milord, must have heard every night for the last eighteen years.

COUNT

And what next?

SCHWARTZ

Several hours later, and as if despite myself, I returned to the cellar. I had the strength to go there certain only of finding a cadaver, and I observed the child healthy and full of life—it smiled and extended its arms to me. God wanted it to live. Could I kill it, Milord Count? I shouted to myself: let the will of God be done. I made him a cradle of straw and clothes, and each night, I returned to bring him a little nourishment. Thus I saw him grow, saw him suffer, and wept over him, and I loved him—for all these sufferings were my doing. I've loved him for his eighteen years of tears and sorrows—for he's eighteen. Milord Count. He's no longer a child—he's a man, a man you would kill, you hear? You see plainly now why I must not leave, why you mustn't wall up the door, Milord?

COUNT

And I, too, I held in my hands the life of a man, and I, too, showed myself generous, because that man in a fit of jealousy had killed my best friend, and that paper I placed before your eyes was the declaration of the victim—that paper was signed by the dying man, before two witnesses. I took pity on the wife and children of the guilty man, and the guilty man, you have not forgotten, was your father.

SCHWARTZ

Yes, my father whose life and honor cost his poor son dearly. Oh, blessed be those who know, respected by all, father—for those blessings and the respect which surrounded you has been paid for by your son's repose, his honor, and the salvation of his soul.

FRITZ

(dressed as a postilion)

Milord Count, the carriage is ready, and here's Herman and his workers.

SCHWARTZ

Already.

(in a whisper)

Master, master—you will retract that order, right? You don't want me to leave, you don't want him to die, right?

COUNT

Enough, enough—

SCHWARTZ

(on his knees)

Oh, I embrace your knees— Listen, let him live—milord, he's unaware of your secret—and how could he betray you, he whose tongue can barely stammer a few words, he who only knows how to ask for a bit of bread, and who calls me his father? Well, this secret that I alone know, you can bury it with me in the tomb. Kill me, kill me if you like, so long as I have no crime, so long as I don't have his death to reproach myself with.

COUNT

(to Herman who comes forward)

Wall up this door!

SCHWARTZ

Stop!

COUNT

(showing him a paper)

Think of your father!

SCHWARTZ

Think of God!

CURTAIN

ACT II

The stage represents an old tower whose open base allows the vault whose exit was seen in the first act to be seen. Some steps lead to this exit, locked by a great gate. There's no light in the vault—some bales of hay form Casper's bed; his crude clothes barely cover him. This vault occupies only a part of the stage, the other part is occupied by the park. The vault is situated under the terrace. The terrace is reached from the park, which borders the exterior wall of the vault by a ruined stairway. Characters coming from the château come down the stairway from the terrace. Characters coming from outside also reach there by the terrace, but come from the right. Near the audience, a small gate giving on the country.

AT RISE, Casper, stretched out on his straw, is in a deep sleep. Dawn has hardly begun. The outside area is still in darkness. Schwartz soon appears, opening the gate to the right; after carefully assuring himself that he is alone, after having climbed the staircase to examine and search the park with his gaze, he comes back down.

SCHWARTZ

At last I'm here. Everyone's still asleep. I've calculated everything. Hardly had Fritz seen me enter the Château of Risburg, then he turned back to return to Ranspach, and yet here I am before him. Indeed, now there's the place I was surprised eighteen years ago, when I was carrying the child; the air hole of the cellar into which I threw my burden, and that ever since I've kept shut in myself—it must be here.

(groping around)

The hedge has grown since that time, and I'm having trouble finding it. No, no—there's the stone that I sealed—it's whiter than the others—let's start to work.

(with his dagger he unseals the stone)

Count de Ranspach, I will thwart your plans and I will cheat your pitiless hate. There were two exits from this vault. You had one walled up—I'll reopen the other one. If God permits it, before anyone comes to surprise me, I will have overcome that obstacle, I will have carried off Casper in my arms to the house of Buttler where I left my horse. Buttler's devoted to me, he'll keep quiet. Casper will remain there for the rest of the day. Tonight—tonight I'll lead him to some out-of-the-way village on the road, where with the gold I'll give him, I will assure him a life that won't be an anticipated death— This stone is giving way to my efforts—it's going to fall— Didn't I hear something? I'm mistaken, no doubt. No one can be crossing the park at this hour. Still, I make out the noise of steps. They're coming from this direction. Could someone have followed me? Spied? Buttler—would he betray me?

(He hides behind a thick copse. A servant enters escorting Frederic.)

FREDERIC

(on the terrace)

And the crisis has lasted a long while?

SERVANT

No, doctor—but very violent, and Miss Mina wanted someone to go inform you.

FREDERIC

Poor woman.

(He disappears with the servant)

SCHWARTZ

It's the young doctor. The day's beginning to come on—and it will require another hour of work to reach Casper! My God, it's you who inspired me with the good thought that brings me here, It's you who said to me: "At the peril of your life, save this child." My God—help me.

(at this moment the sound of a clock is heard)

It's the clock of the great gate. Doubtless it's Fritz returning. All the people of the château are rising, all the windows are opening. From one moment to the next I will be surprised; the Count will be informed and I shall have ruined the one I wanted to save— I must wait until the next night. Prudence demands it. Poor Casper—another day of suffering. For some additional hours the tortures of hunger! But tonight, Casper, I will give you bread, air, and freedom.

(He leaves by the small gate)

CASPER

(in the vault, rousing himself pitifully, and stretching out his hands to find the food that Schwartz ordinarily places there—then in a weak voice)

Father—father.

(He rises, and following the wall which he touches with his hands to guide him, he arrives at the door)

Ah! Father—father, oh, Casper's hungry. Quite hungry.

(Carrying his hands to his breast and his head)

Oh—Casper is ill—here—here.

(scratching the door with his hands)

Father—father—some bread. Some bread.

(wearied by the effort he's just made, Casper collapses on the steps which lead to his door.)

FREDERIC

(emerging from the château, crossing the terrace, and coming down the stairway near the bench, after having glanced around him, sits down)

It's right here that Mina told me to wait for her. I left the Baroness' apartment. I left her more calm. Mina followed me, she sent away the servant who showed me the way, and grasping me by the arm she cast these words in my ear. "Frederic, I must speak to you at the bottom of the terrace; wait for me."

Does Mina actually offer me this herself, she who refused my prayers to meet twenty times? Does Mina actually consent to hear me alone speaking to her of my tenderness? I need a sweet word from Mina. I need to meet her pure and beautiful eyes, to rest my heart and my gaze from the sad spectacle that is offered me here. Poor Baroness—I shall see her die without the power to battle with the grave for her. Her sorrow is not one of those that science can cure or calm.

Someone's coming—it's Mina.

(Mina comes down the stairs rapidly; she seems greatly agitated.)

FREDERIC

(going to her)

Mina!

MINA

Ah, I thank you, Frederic, for having waited for me.

FREDERIC

What's wrong with you, Mina? What's this trouble, this terror depicted in your features?

MINA

I imagined that someone followed me from the château.

FREDERIC

Well, Mina, even if someone found the two of us here, what are you afraid of? Everyone knows that I love you and that the pastor approves of my love for his daughter.

MINA

Shush, Frederic. It's not to hear protestations of that love that I came.

FREDERIC

What are you saying?

MINA

I love you, Frederic, you know it, you've seen my happiness when my father, placing my hand in yours, said to me: "It's a good man—in two years he'll be your husband." Since that day my thoughts have been entirely of this future that is promised us.

FREDERIC

What's occurred in your life—so innocent, so calm, that preoccupies you to this degree, that being alone with Frederic, that having something else to say to him than these very sweet words that he never tires of hearing, "My Frederic, I love you"?

MINA

My friend, since yesterday, I've become certain that in this château there's another person besides my godmother who is ill and crying.

FREDERIC

Who is she?

MINA

I don't know—but the Baroness at least can still breathe pure air, look at the Sun, shake the hands of those who pity and cherish her—while the other unfortunate languishes and is dying in an obscure dungeon whose thick walls intercept his cries and intercept complaint.

FREDERIC

It could be!

MINA

Yesterday, I came alone to sit on this bench, I was thinking of you, Frederic, so kind, so attentive to my poor godmother. Night having fallen, everyone had gone in—the most profound silence reigned. Suddenly, it seemed to me that from this wall escaped muffled moans. First, I believed I was the plaything of an illusion; still, I went closer, and I heard weak and stifled cries—but they must be terrible and lacerating, since they reached me through this thick wall. In the first moment, I wanted to call—warn everybody—but I remembered that this vault was part of the vaults of the tomb whose entrance, yesterday, the Count had walled up. I remembered they had surprised Schwartz heading toward this vault in the middle of the night. Then a terrible thought came to me. It could be that some wretch was shut up in this sepulcher by order of the Count, and I resolved to speak of it only to you. Frederic, what shall we do?

FREDERIC

We will be quiet about what you have discovered, and we will save the one who's condemned by executioners.

MINA

Oh! Yes, that's it, Frederic, we will save him, but how to get to him?

FREDERIC

Hold on—this wall is old. The weight of the earth it supports has broken some of the stones—see, in some place this wall threatens ruin.

MINA

Indeed.

FREDERIC

Perhaps, by removing this foliage—

(He finds the stone partly loosened by Schwartz)

Hold on—this stone is half-loosed, and this is not the work of time but actually of man.

MINA

Perhaps the poor prisoner is working at his deliverance.

FREDERIC

Mina, go up the terrace and watch that no one surprises me—and with the aid of this spade forgotten by the gardener, I'm going to tear out this stone.

MINA

That's it—courage—it's a good deed we are doing. Courage!

(Mina goes up to the terrace and Frederic sets to work)

FREDERIC

It's strange—it seems that the work I'm undertaking has been begun already—this stone wasn't loosened from the inside.

(Casper makes a gesture)

MINA

(from the terrace)

Well?

FREDERIC

As I told you, the wall is in ruins. A few seconds more. Don't you see anyone?

MINA

Nobody.

(Casper rises as if revived by the noise Frederic is making; too weak to walk, he drags himself to the side from which the noise is coming.)

COUNT

Father—father.

FREDERIC

(stopping suddenly)

Mina!

MINA

What's wrong?

FREDERIC

I heard the voice of the prisoner—it reached me.

(low)

We're coming to help you. Hope! Hope!

(Casper, trying to rise, leans on the wall for support.)

CASPER

Bread—bread.

FREDERIC

(in a low voice)

The poor unfortunate! One moment more and this obstacle which separates us will have given way to my efforts. So as not to leave any tracks, I am going to cast these disturbed stones into your cell. Watch out.

(Frederic makes a last effort, and several stones, violently loosened, are pushed back into the vault, but they strike and knock down Casper who falls uttering a scream. Mina comes down at the noise. Frederic joyfully shows her the breach he's just made that permits him to enter the vault.)

I've succeeded, Mina, I've succeeded!

MINA

Oh, my God, it's you who's led me here.

FREDERIC

I don't hear anything more. Whoever you may be, fear nothing. We are the liberators that Heaven's sending you.

MINA

No response. Those last groans were groans of agony. Perhaps, the unfortunate is dead.

FREDERIC

I'm going to assure myself of it.

MINA

(with terror)

Frederic! Oh, don't go in there!

FREDERIC

Mina, we promised God to save this unfortunate—let me finish what we so happily began.

(With effort Frederic enters the vault. Light penetrates the breach, guides him, and soon reveals to him Casper, who's fainted.)

There he is! He's a young man—almost a child—these falling stones injured him. His face is bloodied.

MINA

(with terror)

Ah, my God!

FREDERIC

(tearing off a swatch of Casper's clothes, and staunching the blood)

Don't worry, Mina—he's only fainted because his heart's still beating beneath my hand. This cordial that I brought for the Baroness—

(He shakes it)

MINA

Hurry, hurry, Frederic— I am trembling for him now. Ah, my God, someone's coming from that direction, Frederic, someone's coming—if it's the Count, you are lost.

FREDERIC

Push the branches of the shrubbery back—they'll hide the breach. Be mistress of yourself.

MINA

Come, and let's get out of here instead.

FREDERIC

No, no—I won't leave here except with this unfortunate.

(going back into the dungeon)

Because she said it—we are doing a good deed.

MINA

(replacing the shrubbery)

May God's will be done!

(at this moment the Count, who seems enshrouded in his thoughts, slowly descends from the terrace.)

It's the Count— O my courage, don't abandon me!

(Mina places herself in front of the shrubbery. In the vault Frederic has placed Casper's head on his knees and tries to make him swallow drops of the cordial)

COUNT

What are you doing here, Mina?

MINA

Me, Milord? I—

COUNT

Do you think the Baroness can remain so long deprived of our cares? She's asking for you of everyone? Get going—

MINA

(aside)

Abandon Frederic?

COUNT

Didn't you hear me?

MINA

Pardon me, I'm waiting for you, Milord—without doubt you are also going back to the Baroness.

COUNT

(sitting on the bench)

No—your presence will be much more agreeable to her than mine. I'll stay here.

MINA

(aside)

Frederic is lost—what to do?

COUNT

I told them to inform me as soon as Fritz arrives. Remember that order. Have them find me.

MINA

In the grand avenue?

COUNT

No—here. Go.

MINA

(aside)

Let's run and warn my father. He's the pastor if this county, he is respected even by the Count. In front of him he won't dare commit a new crime. My God, protect Frederic until my return.

(Mina leaves running, the Count remains buried in his thoughts)

FREDERIC

(in the vault)

The cordial recalled a life almost extinguished. Some

moments more and the unfortunate will be able to speak to us. I no longer hear Mina's voice. She's led the Count away, no question.

(Frederic rises, goes to the breach; as he is about to move the foliage, he notices the Count and moves back hurriedly to the vault.)

He's there! Alone!

COUNT

Since yesterday, I don't know where to find a refuge from myself. Last night, at my bedside, just now, near my daughter, even here, I think I hear the agony of the wretch I condemned. The sight of the Baroness was a torture to me. It was only for a moment, during a break in her sorrow. Mina was smiling. She smiled at something near her feet. Her child. Ah, it was horrible.

FREDERIC

(who's gone close to Casper)

He shivered. If he speaks, the two of us are lost.

COUNT

The action that I committed is a crime. But I alone must bear the weight of it! Yours, Leone, yours was most of this crime. Ah, why didn't you accept my challenge? My hate would have assuaged itself in your blood, and perhaps, I'd have been merciful to your son. But today my daughter has a spouse who will demand an account from her of the shame engraved on his name.

CASPER

(beginning to come to himself, making a gesture)

Father—what do you want of me?

FREDERIC

(placing his hand over his mouth)

Shush, wretch, shush.

COUNT

(rising)

Didn't I hear?

(a valet appears on the terrace)

What do you want of me?

VALET

Following your orders, Milord, I am coming to announce to you the arrival of—

COUNT

Of Fritz?

VALET

Yes, Milord, he's entering the Grand Court.

COUNT

That's fine—let him go up to my office.

(The Valet leaves)

Schwartz is at Risburg, no question. He'll never come back to Ranspach. He must leave Austria—I no longer wish to see this man.

(The Count goes and crosses the terrace; at the same moment, Mina and her father enter from the park.)

MINA

Come, come, father.

KLAUS

But I don't see the Count.

MINA

My God! Could we have arrived too late? Frederic,

Frederic—it's me, it's Mina!

FREDERIC

Mina—and you, too, Pastor Klaus. Don't worry, the Count has seen nothing, heard nothing—but we've got to hurry, we've got to lead the unfortunate who owes us his life far from here. Help me, Mr. Klaus, and you, Mina, keep watch.

(Helped by Klaus, Frederic drags Casper out of the vault and places him momentarily on the bench. Casper's face is frightfully pale. His ragged clothes barely cover him. His disordered hair almost covers his shoulders.)

FREDERIC

(aside)

We must get him out of here before he comes to.

KLAUS

We will take him to my place. This is a horrible secret we've discovered.

MINA

Poor young man!

(Frederic intends to cover Casper with Klaus's cloak, but Casper, whose senses revive, rejects the cloak.)

CASPER

Father—father!

MINA

Don't worry, we'll save you.

(Casper opens his eyes on hearing Mina's voice. The light blinds him—he stands up abruptly—remaining quite astonished to see. The violence of his action, the strangeness of his looks, terrify Mina, who hides behind Klaus. As for Casper, he tries to endure the sight of heaven. He points with joy to the rays of Sun that light up the park. He admires all that surrounds him. With the curiosity of a child he touches the trees, the shrubs. Then, noticing Mina, he lets out a cry of surprise, looks at her, admires her, and runs to her. Mina recoils. Frederic places himself in front of her. At the sight of Frederic, Casper stops, looks at him attentively as if he wanted to recognize him, and in a questioning tone, says timidly)

CASPER

Father—father!

MINA

You'll never go back to that cell again. You're going to come with us—with us.

(Finally, Casper understands that he's going to follow Frederic)

(Casper lends his ear to Frederic's voice, as if to recognize that of Schwartz)

FREDERIC

(to Klaus)

That's the only word he says.

(to Casper)

I am only your liberator.

(Casper is motionless)

You are free. Freedom—it's the air that you breathe, it's the Sun whose rays are lighting you and warming you. My God—he doesn't understand me. Freedom—it's an eternal goodbye to this dungeon which you'll never go back to.

(Frederic has pointed to the vault. Casper runs to the breach and recognizes the vault. Distancing himself from it immediately with terror, and falling to his knees, he shouts in a lacerating voice.)

CASPER

Oh, oh—there Casper was really cold, Casper was

really hungry.

MINA

You'll never go back to that cell again. You're going to come with us—with us.

(Finally Casper understands that he's going to follow Frederic and Mina; his joy explodes, he kisses the hands of Frederic and Mina, then his chest inflates, his breathing becomes short and difficult.)

FREDERIC

This emotion is too violent for him. His mind is wandering.

(Casper indeed has a paroxysm of joy—he runs around as if mad, weeping and laughing all at once, a nervous trembling seizes him, he falls down near the vault, and to get away from it, he drags himself to Mina and faints at her feet.)

KLAUS

It's necessary to profit by this faint, and the night that's falling. Cover him with this cloak. If we meet anyone, we'll say he is a poor sick person that we're taking to the presbytery.

MINA

That's it—

KLAUS

Whatever happens, children, I beg you never to reveal what we know of this horrible secret. We will invent a story to avoid suspicion. God will forgives us a lie that must save an innocent head.

FREDERIC.

Let's leave, let's leave, and you, Mina, return to the château—your absence will be noticed.

MINA

I obey you. I will go to see you tomorrow. My God, watch over them.

(Frederic and Klaus carry out Casper, and disappear by way of the terrace. Mina goes back into the Château. The stage remains empty for a moment; night comes on. The small gate opens and Schwartz appears.)

SCHWARTZ

No one— Let's finish the work.

(he runs to the shrubs, pushes them back, and recoils at noticing the breach)

Ah, they've discovered everything.

(rushing to the vault)

Casper, Casper—it's me—it's father.— No response. The Count must have learned everything. He must have found another accomplice.

(looking around again)

Nothing, nothing.

(he picks up the shred of clothing that Frederic used to staunch Casper's blood)

Blood—blood.

It can't be doubted any longer. They've murdered him.

(falling to his knees)

My God, my God—it's not on my head that this blood must fall back on one day.

CURTAIN

ACT III

Houses on the outskirts of the village of Morat. On one side, the dwelling of the pastor, on the other, the entrance to the cemetery. At the back, an avenue leading to the forest. Several peasants enter the cemetery. Others watch them, hat in hand.

1st PEASANT

He was a brave and worthy man.

2nd PEASANT

Yes, he was esteemed, he was respected.

SARA

(entering)

Poor old man, he often gave alms to the little beggar girl—and yet he wasn't rich.

ALL

It's Sara.

SARA

Well, yes, it's me.

1st PEASANT

Where are you coming from?

SARA

From the forest, picking up tinder wood. By the way—say—I saw him.

1st PEASANT

Who?

SARA

The handsome young man.

A WOMAN

What handsome young man?

SARA

The one who came here, one night, no one knows from where—and who for such a long while has been carefully hidden in the home of the Pastor. Yesterday, he escaped the surveillance of his doctor, Mr. Frederic—he was all alone in the forest.

A WOMAN

You spoke to him?

SARA

Right away.

1st PEASANT

She must have asked him for alms.

SARA

Heck! It was necessary. Besides, he had such a gentle manner that I was encouraged.

WOMAN

What did he give you?

SARA

Nothing—oh, why, I don't care. I am sure that he's a kind young man, He didn't seem to understand what I was asking of him. He took the hand that I was extending toward him and he clasped it in his, smiling at me. Then without saying a single word to me, he continued on his way.

2nd PEASANT

Why, who can he be?

ALL

Yes, yes—who can he be?

FRITZ

(appearing suddenly in the midst of the group)

Who's that?

1st PEASANT

What?

FRITZ

You said, "Who could he be?" And as for me, I said—"Who's that?"

2nd PEASANT

What's that to you?

SARA

Eh—it's Mr. Fritz, the Count's footman.

ALL

The Count?

FRITZ

No question. I'm coming to prepare lodgings in the Château de Morat that we haven't visited for quite a long while, and where we are coming, Madame the Baroness, The Count, and myself, to spend a few days. The Count and his daughter are coming ahead of the Baron—the son-in-law who's coming from Vienna. You see plainly that I am no stranger here, and that I have the right to ask: who's that?

SARA

Well, we were speaking of a very mysterious young man, who came here several months ago with Mr. Frederic and Mina, his cousin.

FRITZ

(forcefully)

I know—

ALL

Ha, ha.

FRITZ

I know Doctor Frederic and his cousin, Miss Mina.

SARA

Well, the young man—

FRITZ

He's a complete stranger to me. But he's got some mystery about him which excites my curiosity. It will also excite the curiosity of the Count—who's very curious.

(aside)

I am going to mention it to him while removing his boots—that will increase the favor I'm enjoying.

SARA

Ah! There's Miss Mina.

MINA

Yes, it's me, my friends, coming to entreat you to—What do I see—Fritz?

FRITZ

Myself, Madame Mina.

MINA

And my godmother? Quick, give me news of her.

FRITZ

She's better, much better Miss. She speaks of you quite often, and was saying that you had left to care for your uncle. How is your uncle?

SARA

Our pastor. He only has gout and he's never been ill.

FRITZ

(aside)

Oh—oh! So that's why he's so long getting better.

MINA

(excitedly)

My uncle has kept me—

FRITZ

And Mr. Frederic, too.

MINA

But I'm counting on leaving soon, I'm eager to see my

godmother again.

FRITZ

No need to disturb yourself about that—because Madame's coming to Morat.

MINA

They allowed her to make the trip? Her strength has finally returned—and she's coming alone?

FRITZ

Absolutely alone.

MINA

(with joy)

Ah!

FRITZ

With her father.

MINA

(with terror)

The Count!

FRITZ

(aside)

This is singular—how the air of him gives pleasure. But I am here, I'm chatting, and Milord awaits me.

(aloud)

Goodbye, Miss Mina.

There's some mystery about this. I'll inform the Count all about it.

(Fritz leaves)

MINA

(aside)

The Count is so near Casper.

(aloud)

My friends, you know that our young patient has need of great consideration. He's going to come out, and the sight of so many people—

1st PEASANT

That suffices, Miss—we're leaving.

(aside)

It's over—she doesn't want anyone to come near him.

(The peasants move away, slowly casting curious glances at the pastor's door—which only opens after everyone has left.)

MINA

(alone)

Is it only chance that brings the Count here— To accompany Casper, who at all costs had to distance himself from Ranspach, Frederic and I concocted a grave illness of my uncle—Fritz won't fail to say what he's just discovered. The Count is suspicious—and wary—and wants to know the whole truth.

How to hide Casper from his eyes. What to reply when he questions us.

(to Frederic who enters)

Where is Casper?

FREDERIC

(pointing)

There.

MINA

You left him alone?

FREDERIC

No question. Casper is no longer that puny creature we saved. His long compromised intelligence has developed with a prodigious ardor. What we have not yet been able to teach him, he senses or divines. If sometimes a wild nature awakens at some ancient memory—a word, and an act of his friends, calms him and appeases him; he's a man still a child. But he's a man. We no longer have anything to fear for him.

MINA

Oh—you are mistaken, Frederic. Know that the Count and the Baroness are arriving this very day at the Château de Morat—where they've not visited for the last two years.

FREDERIC

The Count! The Count at Morat!

MINA

Perhaps he already knows the reason behind our departure from Ranspach and of our stay here.

FREDERIC

Who would have informed him?

MINA

Fritz, who just now learned that my uncle's illness has only been pretended.

FREDERIC

Far from being frightened by peril, it must be confronted. I will run to the castle, I will tell the Count all he can know of the truth. It's impossible for us now to hide Casper's existence from him. I will tell him what we've already told your uncle. If the Count wants to see Casper, he shall see him. The memories of our friend are so vague, so confused, that the Count will be unable to find a reasonable basis for his suspicions.

(Casper emerges from the house; he's no longer the Casper of the previous act; a simple but graceful costume has replaced the ragged clothes which covered him. His gaze is more calm, his voice more assured, and more gentle. There's still naivety in his features and in his tone, but no more idiocy.)

CASPER

Mina! Frederic!

(going to them)

It's quite a long while since you left me.

(taking their hands)

It's when I'm holding your two hands in mine that I am happy. When one of you leaves me, it's half my happiness that's leaving— You told me that it was God who gave us life. Am I living in this horrible night from which you dragged me? Life—why it's to see, hear, feel, and it's through you that I see, that I sense, that I hear—life is the beautiful heaven that floods me with its light, it's this pure air that refreshes my face, and it's you who gave me all that.

What has this God that you adore done for Casper? Mina, Frederic, my God, my religion, my belief—it's you.

MINA

All that's been done, Casper, was accomplished by the will of this God you doubt—of this God that I pray to every day for you. And this evening, my prayers will be more fervent still—for a new danger threatens you.

CASPER

(who hasn't understood, moves away to admire the flowers in front of the pastor's door.)

Look, will you, Mina. How beautiful these flowers are.

(He doesn't listen)

FREDERIC

He hasn't understood you, Mina. But I'm running to get ahead of this danger.

(Frederic leaves)

(Casper sits down on a bench near some of Mina's flowers)

MINA

(looking at him)

He doesn't understand that they want his freedom and his life. Of this world he still only knows the good.

(going to him)

Casper, my friend, you must go back inside!

CASPER

Go back in so soon? Oh, no, rather come with me into this beautiful forest that yesterday I was exploring alone.

MINA

What imprudence!

CASPER

It's yesterday that I felt truly free. Yet, for a moment I was afraid. Yes, the thick foliage of these great trees hid the sight of the Sun from me. I thought I was falling back into the night of my tomb, a rock was in front of me, I scaled it to get closer to the Sun I could no longer see. Oh, Mina, Mina, reaching the height of the rock, those trees that were imprisoning me were beneath my feet, above my head, nothing—not a thing! A whole world, an infinite space that my glance devoured. I would like to be able to tell you all that took place in my soul, but I don't know; I barely know words that describe thoughts. With shouts of joy rushing from my breast, with tears rolling from my eyes—yes—I wept—and I was happy—quite happy to live.

At last I fell on my knees.

MINA

To pray?

CASPER

No, because I don't know how to pray. But because before this immense space, before thse unknown marvels, I dared not remain standing.

MINA

Well, Casper—these marvels, this world—all this is

the work of God.

CASPER

What I experienced yesterday I had once tried before; yes, that was the day when suddenly emerged from nothingness, I found myself before you, Mina—and I remember that before you, too, I fell to my knees.

(Casper kneels before Mina who is seated on the bench. She wants to rise and go inside, but Casper holds her back.)

Oh, let's stay longer, let's await Frederic's return. This morning, Frederic was near you, as I am here—from there—

(pointing to the windows)

I saw the two of you. You seemed quite happy listening to him. And, as for me, I was very happy for your happiness.

Frederic was saying to you, "Mina, my reward is in your love." But what did Frederic mean, Mina? I didn't understand him.

MINA

You must ask him.

CASPER

This is the first time that Mina has refused to reply to Casper!

MINA

I'm wrong, Casper, I'm wrong! Love is a chaste feeling and pure, that we ought to admit, because it's God who put it in one's heart. True love is the riches of the poor, the consolation of the orphan; for it, the saddest past is forgotten, the most somber future is embellished—true love is a second life in life. You'll experience this feeling one day. The young girl who will have inspired it in you will have all your thoughts; when she speaks, you will love to listen to the sound of her voice, when your hand touches hers, your heart will leap with joy in your breast, and this holy and sacred love fire will only extinguish with your life. Now that's the love that Frederic was speaking of this morning.

CASPER

(who has devoured Mina with his eyes while she was speaking seems to experience all the sensations that that she analyzed. Casper rises, saying)

Mina! Mina!

(at this moment Frederic enters.)

FREDERIC

Mina, I've seen the Count and The Baroness. I've spoken to them of Casper and his misfortunes. Madame will come this very day to see Casper—in whom she's already interested; no doubt, the Count will accompany her.

(Going to Casper, who's remained thoroughly pensive)

My friend, you must go in.

CASPER

Why?

FREDERIC

To prepare you for an interview on which your destiny may depend.

MINA

Come, Casper, and follow all Frederic's advice.

(All three enter the pastor's home)

SCHWARTZ

(descends excitedly from the hillock, and stops before the small house at the right)

Morat! At last I am in Morat! Here's the house of my father, of my old father, for whom I no longer have anything to worry about. The fatal evidence which could ruin and wither his old age, I've got it here, by my heart.

(falling on a bank of grass)

Let's wait a moment before rapping on the door. Let's gather some strength for joy! The Count no longer wishes to see me again—the pitiless man fears blushing and lowering his eyes before me. He sent these papers to me at Risburg, which he no longer needs to assure my silence. Casper, finally fallen under his blows—what has he to fear from me?—and has rendered me my freedom. Poor Casper! O my father! My father, to you all the life that remains to me. Go.

(Schwartz raps on the door; no one responds)

No one. The old geezer is doubtless seated at the foot of one of these trees, asking the Sun to heat his freezing blood? Which way to direct my steps?

(Peasants leave the cemetery. Schwartz looks at them and runs to them.)

Perhaps these men will tell me.

(noticing that the peasants are emerging from the cemetery)

Ah—someone in Morat has died.

1st PEASANT

Yes, and a brave man.

SCHWARTZ

An old friend of mine, perhaps?

1st PEASANT

So you are from around here?

SCHWARTZ

Yes. Schwartz is my father.

2nd PEASANT

Oh—he's the son of old Schwartz!

SCHWARTZ

The name, the name of the one you've just escorted to his final resting place, tell me? If he's childhood friend, I wish like you, to honor his tomb.

1st PEASANT

(low)

I'll never dare to tell him.

2nd PEASANT

(stopping a peasant crossing the stage)

You ask the name of the poor deceased? Here, you might read it on the cross that Frantz is going to place down there.

SCHWARTZ

(watching them all)

Why are they looking at me like this? Why is it my heart is shaking? Give me, give me this cross.

(hesitating, they give it to him, and all watch as Schwartz passes his hand over his face, then looks and reads.)

Schwartz! Oh! Oh!

(rubs his eyes, then reads again)

Schwartz! Oh, tell me that I am in delirium! Tell me— You are silent! My father! My father!

PEASANT

(removing his hat and pointing to the cemetery)

He's been there since this morning.

SCHWARTZ

Oh! Oh! My poor father! Dead—dead without having seen his son again! Without having embraced him! Dead! And I was coming with a heart full of joy! And nothing, nothing told me on the way that the most frightful of misfortunes was awaiting me here. Take me there, take me there, so that I can at least kiss the ground that's covering him! He'll hear my cries, he will hear my last goodbye! Or rather, no, no—leave me, I will go alone. Oh, among all these tombs I will recognize his! Leave me alone, leave me alone.

(Schwartz falls on his knees before the cross that he holds in his hands; the peasants silently distance themselves. Still on his knees)

O my father! No longer to see you again— And never be able to tell you all the love there was for you in this heart. My father, you left this world without knowing to what horrible torture your son condemned himself for you! Who now will relieve me of my crime? Who now will efface from my face the blood stain that Casper has left there? Oh, Casper! Casper!

(The window in the pastor's house opens and Casper appears there.)

CASPER

Someone said my name.

SCHWARTZ

Oh, I will not survive all those I loved.

CASPER

(with a great reaction)

That's his voice.

SCHWARTZ

To my father, to Casper.

CASPER

(emerging from the house and seeing Schwartz)

Father! Father!

SCHWARTZ

(rising in terror)

Casper! Casper! No, it's impossible.

CASPER

Father, don't you recognize me? Oh, I really recognized your voice—that voice which called me in the night of my tomb, that voice—the only one I was permitted to hear.

SCHWARTZ

It's him, it's him—Casper—he's alive, my god, he's alive. Oh, you have taken pity on me, Lord. You have tailored my misfortunes to my strengths, you have taken my father from me, but you've given him back to me. He's alive.

(embracing Casper)

Yes, it's really you, my Casper, my child!

CASPER

(distancing himself)

You aren't coming to take me away from my friends, are you? You are not coming to tear me away from the world, from light, from life?

SCHWARTZ

No, no! Oh, you're afraid of me. That's just. You must hate me, that's just, too. I was pressing you in my arms, but it's at the knees of the victim that the executioner must fall.

(Schwartz kneels)

CASPER

(raising him up)

What are you doing? Me, hate you? Oh, I know what these words hate and love mean, and I love you, do you really hear, father? I love you. In the confusion of my memories, one alone remained with me. It's yours. In the midst of all this commotion around me, I still hear your voice. Father, you were capable of believing in my hate, but who nourished me? It was you. Who warmed me in his arms? It was you. I haven't forgotten him, my enemy, the one who I ought to hate, he's the one who condemned me to never see the day—but that one is not you. Oh, no, no—my heart tells me that wasn't you.

SCHWARTZ

No, no—that one said to me, "Slave, kill this child or I will kill your father." But heaven didn't want to crush me under the weight of an eternal remorse. Heaven saved you from my servile obedience. I hid you in the bowels of the earth for eighteen years. I nourished you with most of my bread, I covered you with most of my clothes, and if I didn't give you freedom and sunlight, it's because my father would have paid with his life for your deliverance. But the new protectors that God has sent you have left me a task to accomplish; they freed you, Casper; I will make you happy. I will pay you for your eighteen years of tortures and anguish, and to do that child, I will give you back your mother.

CASPER

My mother!

SCHWARTZ

Your new friends must have taught you that your mother was a holy and sacred treasure. If she still exists, I will return her to you, I tell you, and pressed to her heart, covered with caresses, you will forget all that Schwartz has done to make you suffer. When you were placed in my hands, I found this bracelet, precious indicia that your mother had placed on your heart. Heavens, there it is, this bracelet!

CASPER

Give it to me, give it to me. It comes from my mother, it will never leave me.

SCHWARTZ

Now, Casper, for Schwartz, go begin a new life, and that one, I hope, will repurchase the other. As of today, we will leave, we will go to Vienna, yes, I, poor man of the people, I will go if needs be to the Emperor; I will tell him your misfortunes. I will tell him the hate of your persecutor, I will say to him. "You are all powerful, after God, I confide this child to you, protect him." And as for me, with this bracelet that you will return to me then, I will scour, if needs be, all

Germany—heaven will lead me to the mother who's weeping for her child. I will say to her, "He's alive, he's waiting for you, come, the Emperor and the law are protecting him for you."

CASPER

Yes, yes, that's it, we'll leave. But Frederic, Mina—no longer to see them again—oh—it's that I love them, too.

SCHWARTZ

I will tell them what I want to do for you. They will approve, because they will understand that you will never be safe except under the Imperial aegis. It's there in that house that your friends live—go await me with them. Before leaving this country, I have a duty to fulfill. Father, I wanted to give you these funereal papers that I paid for so dearly. I will tear them up on your tomb. Casper, your pure and naïve prayer will reach the throne of the Eternal! Poor child, pray for the father of Schwartz who died without having embraced his son.

(Casper kneels, then Schwartz goes into the cemetery.)

MINA

(entering)

There they are! There they are!

CASPER

Who's that?

FREDERIC

Who's that?

MINA

The Count and the Baroness. From my window I noticed them heading this way. Casper, my friend, they are going to question you—be careful what you say to them.

(Casper without hearing her turns toward the cemetery.)

BARONESS

(entering with the Count)

Frederic, that young man is no question the one you told us about this morning.

FREDERIC

Yes, Madame. It's himself. He's hardly begun life, and already he's suffered a lot.

BARONESS

Him, too.

(to Casper)

Approach! What we know already of you and your misfortunes has sharply touched us, These misfortunes have reached their end, believe it well.

COUNT

Doctor Frederic has told us that he met you alone and lost in the forest of Ranspach—you couldn't explain to him how you found yourself thus abandoned, but today, through the cares of the doctor, your reason has been enlightened, so that today a sweet and happy life must have brought calm to your mind—cannot you pull together some memories, give some indicia which will place us on the track of the truth?

FREDERIC

Milord, Count, when I met this young man, he had not, I repeat to you, any knowledge of himself, he hardly knew how to articulate some words without nonsense and the name of Casper—which we've kept for him.

COUNT

But this name—who gave it to you?

CASPER

He did.

COUNT

Who's he?

CASPER

Father.

FREDERIC

That's the way he designates the man who no doubt raised him, nurtured him.

COUNT

Before knowing Doctor Frederic, had you seen only this man?

CASPER

No one except him.

COUNT

(after a reaction which he controls)

Casper, your memory—is it unfaithful to the degree that you could not tell in what place your childhood unfolded?

FREDERIC

His memories are too confused, too vague for—

COUNT

Let him answer—

MINA

(aside)

My God—what's he going to say?

BARONESS

Speak—speak without fear.

CASPER

Madame, dig up the ground, dig it up before all commotion is silent, so all light is extinguished, make Casper descend into his tomb. You will understand then the dwelling chosen for him.

COUNT

This is strange!

BARONESS

Eh, what! Poor child—you were raised in a dungeon? For eighteen years you didn't see the light of the heavens, you didn't hear the voice of a friend?

CASPER

Oh, yes Madame, I had a friend—he's the one who came every day to bring me my bread, he stayed a little time with me, and I only lived during that time, one time I was waiting for him vainly. Oh, that was my greatest torture—this expectation—suddenly the stones of my vault shook—one of them came falling in and struck me on the head, from that moment I could no longer see. I no longer felt anything—when I came to, I was free—that's all I know, Madame, that's all I am capable of telling you.

COUNT

(aside)

It's him.

BARONESS

Poor Casper! So young and already so much suffering—but I told you, all your misfortunes are over. I won't leave to Miss Mina the gentle mission of making you a new life.

COUNT

(aside)

O Schwartz, Schwartz!

BARONESS

And first of all, you shall never leave us.

COUNT

(aside)

What's she say?

FREDERIC

Madame, I thank you again for your kindness to Casper, but from the moment heaven gave him to me, I named him my brother. Oh, Madame, leave me, leave me my brother.

CASPER

Casper cannot follow the Baroness, he cannot stay with Mina, Casper's going to leave.

ALL

Leave!

COUNT

Where then are you going?

CASPER

Wait—to Vienna, yes, to Vienna.

COUNT

(going to him)

To Vienna—and who will escort you there?

CASPER

Him—father.

COUNT

(excitedly)

You've seen him again?

BARONESS

Then that man could tell us—

COUNT

(trying to correct himself)

Yes, you are right, that man will complete Casper's

revelations. I will question him—but, until then, Casper will stay with us. I am taking him under my protection, and my protection will be more powerful than yours, Frederic. Come then, Casper, from this moment, you are mine, from this moment you must never leave me.

FREDERIC

(aside)

He's intuited everything.

COUNT

Let's go.

(Schwartz has appeared at the gate of the cemetery—noticing the Count, he makes a gesture of surprise and terror—then he cocks his ear. At the moment the Count intends to go take Casper's hand, it's Schwartz's hand that he finds)

SCHWARTZ

One moment, Milord Count. Before you leave this place, before you lead this child away, I must speak to you; send everyone away.

COUNT

But—

SCHWARTZ

(low)

I insist on it!

COUNT

Daughter, my friends, leave me alone with this man.

CASPER

(hugging Schwartz, and pointing him out to the Baroness)

It's him. He's my father!

BARONESS

Him!

MINA

Come—come, Casper.

(Everyone goes into the pastor's home—looking with anxiety at the Count and Schwartz)

COUNT

Schwartz, why didn't you keep your oath?

SCHWARTZ

I didn't fail in it, sir; another hand than mine saved Casper.

COUNT

You lie—you think yourself able to brave me because, weak and trusting, I delivered those papers to you that chained you to me—but my testimony and my credit will still suffice to—

SCHWARTZ

Old Schwartz no longer has anything to fear from you—one only judges the living, and old Schwartz is dead.

COUNT

Dead!

SCHWARTZ

I've just said my last goodbye at his tomb. Twenty years of my life have been dedicated to my father—all the days that heaven is keeping for me now belong to your victim—that I will no longer allow you take back.

COUNT

Listen, Schwartz, our roles are reversed, I see that it's

up to me to entreat—I ask you no longer for Casper's death—that sentence, I would no longer have the strength to pronounce—for the sight of that child has touched my heart. Let him live, but let him live far from Germany. In a few days you will leave with him. I will give you enough gold to render you each rich and happy— What do you care about exile? Casper has no country—you no longer have any family. You will leave with him in three days.

SCHWARTZ

I won't leave.

COUNT

What do you mean?

SCHWARTZ

I've sworn to God and to my father that justice will be done by me—and justice will be done, Milord!

COUNT

Oh, no—you must have pity on me.

SCHWARTZ

Did you have any pity on him, when I was rolling at your feet, asking you for mercy for the child you wanted to immure in the sepulcher? I hugged your knees. I bathed your hands with my tears—that day you rejected me pitilessly. I reject you today. Ah, you said it, our roles are reversed.

COUNT

But what do you want? What do you exact?

SCHWARTZ

Nothing from you. Because you can repair nothing. What can you offer to Casper in exchange for a whole life of torture? Gold! Money! Now, there are actually these powerful folk who imagine one can pay for everything with gold.

I will do much more for Casper, I'll give him back his mother.

COUNT

(terrified)

His mother? Do you know her?

SCHWARTZ

(As if struck by a sudden idea, looking towards where the Baroness has exited)

Perhaps.

COUNT

Wretch! But do you know that before you can make such a revelation, I will have you killed?

SCHWARTZ

(approaching the Count with concentrated rage)

Do you know that the one you are threatening hates you with all the strength of his soul? Do you know that one, feeling his chain break, promised to strike you in the face? Do you know that in the end he has to make you expiate his remorse and Casper's tortures? Don't you see that you are alone with this man and that he has a dagger—

COUNT

(putting his hand near his breast)

Wretch!

SCHWARTZ

You've just inspired me with a terrible thought. You are Casper's evil genius. The hand always suspended over his head—is yours. So long as you live I will have to tremble for Casper, and I no longer wish to fear for him.

Count, the first death threat came from your mouth.

Count, pray God, and may all your blood fall back on me—because you are going to die.

COUNT

(coldly, recoiling a step)

You intend to assassinate me?

SCHWARTZ

I intend to save Casper! On your knees, sir, pray to God.

COUNT

For you perhaps?

(pulling a pistol from his breast he aims it at Schwartz and shoots him in the heart.)

SCHWARTZ

Ah, ah—Casper! Casper!

(Schwartz falls dead)

CASPER

(rushing in)

What a commotion. Father! Father!

(returning to him)

Blood! Blood!

(Casper throws himself on Schwartz's body.)

COUNT

(to everyone)

This wretch raised a dagger against me, his master. I killed him.

(to a servant)

Tell the Burgomaster to come take my deposition.

CASPER

Father—father—

FREDERIC

(examining Schwartz)

His heart's no longer beating. He's dead!

COUNT

(aside)

And he'll take his secret with him to the grave.

CURTAIN

ACT IV

A rich hall in the Castle of Ranspach.

FREDERIC

(going ahead of Mina)

Have you seen Casper?

MINA

No—he's not yet left his room. You know that since the death of the one he called his father, Casper has become somber and suspicious; and my godmother, fearing that the sight of the places where he left his friend would end by separating him from his reason, convinced the Count to leave Morat Château and return to Ranspach.

FREDERIC

And for the last week, Casper has been, without knowing it, in the dwelling which has seen his first and longest sorrows, and where perhaps new persecutions await him.

MINA

Oh, no, it's impossible; what interest can the Count have in torturing our friend thus?

FREDERIC

And what interest has he in also keeping me at a distance from this château?

MINA

He could do that!

FREDERIC

Yes, Mina, yes, he's keeping me away, because now, I alone am the supporter and protector of Casper.

MINA

Oh, you are mistaken, Frederic.

VALET

(entering)

For Mr. Frederic.

(The valet gives him a letter and leaves)

FREDERIC

(reading)

The Court of Vienna has given the order to obtain information as to the birth and captivity of Casper. Mr. Frederic will leave this very day for Vienna, so as to communicate the information he possesses and the observations his art has allowed him to gather.

(To Mina)

You see—we have to separate today—perhaps in a few hours.

MINA

My friend, you cannot resist this order, but in leaving Casper a support, a protector, Frederic you must take everything to my godmother.

FREDERIC

To the Baroness! Yes. He saved her life. And then she will understand if I speak to her of the implacable hate of the Count. You must distance yourself, Mina.

MINA

No. I want to join my prayers to yours.

FREDERIC

Think of it, I am going to speak to the Baroness of a crime of which her father is guilty—it's for her father that she must blush—and for that, one witness is enough.

MINA

Yes, I understand and I'll leave you alone.

(Exit Mina.)

FREDERIC

Poor woman, it's a new pain I'm going to cause her.

BARONESS

You are alone, Frederic, I expected to find Mina with you.

FREDERIC

Indeed, she was here—it was only for a moment, but I sent her away so I could speak to you.

BARONESS

To me?

FREDERIC

Madame, you bear some interest in Casper, right? And you would protect him if a great danger threatened him?

BARONESS

Protect him—but against whom?

FREDERIC

Alas, Madame—do I dare to tell you?

BARONESS

Speak, speak, I insist.

FREDERIC

You know, Madame, that from his birth, Casper met an enemy bent on his ruin; this enemy, more cruel than a murderer, condemned him to slow and cruel sorrows—

BARONESS

And this man, do you know him? Could you have discovered him at last?

FREDERIC

Yes, Madame, I know him. And it wasn't enough for

him to have tortured his victim for eighteen years, and it's not enough since the death of Schwartz, when a sole friend, a sole protector, still remains to poor Casper—he removes him—because he needs his prey to be alone and defenseless, for he fears that his arm trembles, and might weaken if he met two hearts to strike instead of one.

BARONESS

Why, in that case, who is this man?

FREDERIC

(hesitating)

This man—is—

FRITZ (entering)

The Count is waiting for you, Mr. Frederic, in his office—he admits of no delay.

FREDERIC

(low)

You see, Madame—he is pitiless, he's driving me away.

BARONESS

Great God! Casper's persecutor—

FREDERIC

(low and leaving)

He's your father, Madame.

(He leaves with Fritz.)

BARONESS

(very agitated)

My father—it's my father, he said, who's condemned Casper—and Casper is eighteen years old. Oh! My God! My God!

(Casper enters, pale and in great disorder)

CASPER

Mina! Frederic! Save me! Save me!

BARONESS

It's him! In what condition—Casper, my friend—what's the matter with you?

CASPER

(distancing himself from the Baroness)

Where am I? Who are you? Ah, I recognize you,

Madame. You call me your friend, and it's you—you alone who led me here. It's you who said to me, "Have confidence in my father! Follow him!" Your father—why, it's he who killed Schwartz. And this Château belongs to your father, right?

BARONESS

No question.

CASPER

Everything belongs to him—everything—even the vault where air is lacking and life is extinguished. Does he intend to make me go down there again? Oh, Madame, rather get him to kill me—with a single shot—like Schwartz.

BARONESS

Why, what is it you've seen?

CASPER

(looking at her)

Oh, I'm not mistaken. You have no hate for Casper. You won't deceive him—he can tell you everything, like Mina, like Frederic— It's strange—when I am with you I hardly dare to speak to you, and yet I feel that I love you the way I love Frederic and Mina.

BARONESS

Yes—if you could understand all that's taking place in my soul— Oh, why, tell me then what has caused this terror. Speak, speak—!

CASPER

(taking her by the hand and leading her to a window)

Hold on—you see that tall and dark tower down there? Just now I was in the park at the foot of that tower. I was weeping, because I was thinking of Schwartz. A sudden noise made me raise my head; this noise seemed to be caused by a stone that came loose and fell. And this noise shook my heart. I looked around me. It seemed to me that I'd already been in this very place—the sand, the bushes, the trees were engraved there. I'd already seen them.

BARONESS

Ah, continue—continue.

CASPER

I got up—a hedge of greenery was in front of me. I moved it aside with my hands. And I noticed a broken-down wall—and behind the wall—a cell.

BARONESS

A cell!

CASPER

Mine! Mine, Madame!

BARONESS

Yours!

CASPER

Yes, the one where I lived, where I'd suffered so long. Ah, I recognized everything—the door, the tombs, the straw for sleeping. At the sight of this, all my memories came back—all my sufferings reawakened. My reason, enlightened by Frederic and Mina, was lost again. As before, I ran to the door—still locked, as before I called father to help me, as before it seemed to me I heard the noise of his steps. Indeed, someone was walking. The hedge parted abruptly—a man appeared at the entrance to the vault. Beside myself, I ran towards this man, screaming, "Father! Father!" And this man and I at the same time uttered a cry of terror and surprise. That man—was your father.

BARONESS

My father.

CASPER

Ah, at the sight of him, I don't know what secret horror carried me away. My tortures, the death of Schwartz, all came back to my mind. "Executioner of Schwartz," I screamed, "are you coming to see the tomb of Casper?" And I rushed on the Count. I dragged him into the cell. In vain he struggled, in vain he asked for mercy. I could only see the ghost of Schwartz smiling at me. I could hear only the voice of Schwartz shouting to me, "Avenge me!" The Count was knocked down—a stone was in my hand—I raised it over his head.

BARONESS

Wretch!

CASPER

The old geezer made a final effort. "Mercy! Mercy! My son!" he yelled. At this word, at the tone of this entreating voice, I felt my delirium and my furor extinguish. The terrible ghost of Casper had vanished. Before me, I had nothing more than an old man begging me for his life on his knees. I cast the stone I was holding from me, and with a leap I rushed out of the vault.

BARONESS

(whose emotion is complete)

He called you his son. Those words, you actually heard

them?

CASPER

Yes, but he gave me that title to excite my pity—my mother alone can call me her son.

BARONESS

Your mother—and what makes you think she's still alive?

CASPER

How pale you are! The way you are trembling.

BARONESS

Oh—answer me! Answer me! My life itself is completely in what you are going to say. Who spoke to you of your mother?

CASPER

Him! Him! Schwartz, Schwartz—who gave me the means of finding her again.

BARONESS

What means? Get to the point!

CASPER

Oh! What you are asking me I've hidden from Mina herself.

BARONESS

Oh—I'm asking you on my knees!

CASPER

I will tell you everything—but in a whisper. So no one else but you will hear. My mother—she's all my hope of happiness. A jewel was placed on me by her. Schwartz kept it.

BARONESS

It's a bracelet, isn't it? It was a bracelet.

CASPER

It's here—next to my heart.

BARONESS

Oh—give me—give me.

(The Baroness extends her arm. Casper notices the bracelet on the Baroness' arm.)

CASPER

Ah!

BARONESS

What's wrong with you?

CASPER

There it is!

BARONESS

Indeed, it ought to be like this one.

CASPER

(pulling it from his breast)

Here! Here!

BARONESS

Yes, yes! That's actually it! Look! Look! Casper, hairs made this bracelet. These hairs are those of your father—it was his only heirloom—and I—your mother—I shared them with my child.

CASPER

Ah, my mother!

BARONESS

Yes, yes, I am your mother!

CASPER

Ah, ah—my mother.

(Casper falls into her arms)

BARONESS

My child! My child! Unfortunate! When he spoke of his long sorrows, I listened to him almost without terror. I felt a tear roll in my eyes, a tear and nothing more. A tear—and my heart was not broken, no—I pitied him as one pities a stranger—a wretch that one soon forgets—and it was my son! My poor son who had suffered all this. And yet it seemed to me that my soul had intuited your tortures, my son—because for eighteen years I was dying here, myself, while you were dying down there. And it was only six months ago, and it was only on the day of your freedom that I came back to life. Oh, because I was a good mother, because for eighteen years my heart experienced your sorrows! Because six months ago I felt you were living again.

CASPER

Oh, my mother, my mother! How happy I am! I am no longer alone, abandoned by the world! I have a mother!

BARONESS

Someone's coming.

CASPER

(frightened)

Someone's coming—to separate us, perhaps—!

BARONESS

Oh! Fear nothing, my son. A mother is strong to defend her child.

(The Count enters)

CASPER

Him! It's him!

COUNT

Why this fright, Casper? You have nothing to fear from me. Daughter, go away for a few minutes at least; I must speak to this young man—to him alone.

BARONESS

Distance myself? You confide in him? Oh, no, no.

COUNT

I order you to do it, my daughter.

BARONESS

As for me, I refuse to obey you, sir.

COUNT

You would forget—

BARONESS

That I am your daughter? No, sir. But I remember that I am his mother.

CASPER

My mother!

COUNT

(aside)

She knows everything.

BARONESS

I confided my child to you once already.

COUNT

Enough, my daughter: spare me the shame of blushing before you; look at me, there's no more anger, there's no more harshness in my eyes—there are only tears, and in my heart there's only remorse.

BARONESS

O my God! Ought I to believe him?

COUNT

Enough of persecutions, enough of sufferings for this young man; besides—all my hopes, aren't they in him? In only a moment he could have avenged himself. He could have killed me, and yet he spared my life. Humble and suppliant, I am coming now to request that he spare my honor.

BARONESS

Could he do it? You no longer threaten him, no longer wish his death. Oh, father—fear nothing from him. His soul is as generous as that of his father—it's a noble blood that flows in his veins.

COUNT

(going toward Casper)

Casper, those who have taught you what you already

know of this new world for you, those who told you what a mother is—did they tell you what honor is?

CASPER

Honor, yes: Frederic told me of it—for what they call honor men will sacrifice their most cherished affections.

COUNT

That's it: to my honor I sacrificed the repose of my life, the salvation of my soul. Hear me carefully, Casper. The kindness of Heaven has returned your mother to you, and she, like you, is abandoning herself completely to the joy of today without thinking of tomorrow's tears—the joys of the mother are effaced by the terrors of the spouse.

CASPER

I no longer understand you.

BARONESS

What are you going to tell him?

COUNT

The whole truth. Gaspard, your father, dead—without your birth unknown to all being legitimated—in a word, your birth was a crime.

BARONESS

Ah, sir—sir.

COUNT

Since then, my daughter has given her hand to a man that we deceived. Because he knows nothing of the past for which he's going to demand an account of us—and this man is returning today.

CASPER

Today!

COUNT

Do you understand me, Casper? He's coming back, and it is he that the Emperor has entrusted with the duty of discovering the secret of your birth, and the names of your persecutors. Oh, if the dishonor only fell back on me, I wouldn't hesitate and I would say, "The lone, the true culprit—it is I." But this man will ask you who is your mother. And if you name her, that will cover her with shame in the eyes of the world. It will draw on her the vengeance of her husband; that will shrivel the honor of my family—of yours, Casper. Look, I'm at your feet—for my life is nothing, but honor, Casper, the name remains standing after all of us are lying in the tomb. Why, 200 years of hereditary glory; oh, I don't want it to be torn from me, I don't want that!

CASPER

(raising him up)

Oh—don't pray to me like this!

BARONESS

And what do you want from him, sir?

COUNT

His oath to be silent about the secret of his birth, his promise to leave Austria. You will choose yourself the place of his exile—and my fortune will follow him there.

BARONESS

Yet another separation. Oh! Don't hope that I will consent to that, sir. That goes with honor, you say? For honor, perhaps, one gives one's life. But a mother doesn't give up her child.

COUNT

Well then, let your will be accomplished, my daughter. Let scandal and shame enter this Château with your husband. They won't spare my white hair; perhaps they'll spare my body.

BARONESS

What are you saying?

COUNT

I'm saying that in an hour your husband will arrive, and that in an hour your father shall have ceased to live. See this ring? It contains enough poison to kill in a moment.

BARONESS

Ah!

COUNT

You both have the right to be pitiless—because I have had no pity for you.

CASPER

(quickly getting between them)

Stop! Stop! I swear before God, and on honor, that my mother's name will never pass my lips. What I've just learned I'll keep locked in here. If I'm questioned, I'll be found mute and without memory.

COUNT

Oh, Casper!

BARONESS

My son!

CASPER

Don't give me that name— Where must I go? I'm ready.

BARONESS

Oh, I will follow you.

CASPER

No. Your husband's returning, Madame—you must await him.

COUNT

Casper—all that can pay you back for a mother's love and caresses you shall have from me; you will go to France; Frederic will accompany you.

BARONESS

Yes, Frederic—Frederic will be your brother. I am going to see him. To him I can entrust my son, because he already saved you. Casper, I will follow the noble example you have given me. I will also shut my love in here. But God doesn't want this separation to be eternal.

COUNT

Daughter, see Frederic—as for me, I am going to prepare orders for the departure of our child—yes, our child. Oh, you said it, it's a noble blood that flows in his veins.

(The Baroness leaves after having embraced Casper. The Count has shaken his hand)

CASPER

(alone, bursting out)

Alone—I am alone and I'm going to cry again. Poor Casper—you have a mother and you can never give her that name, you have a mother and you must hide your love for her, and you will receive neither her caresses nor her kisses—if she's in pain, you'll be far from her. If you weep, it won't be her hand that will dry your eyes; it won't be her eyes which will bring back joy to your heart. That's the law of the world— Ah, what remains for Casper? Death took Schwartz from him, the world is taking his mother from him. Ah—

(noticing Mina)

Mina!

MINA

Casper—they told me you were with the Count and I

was afraid.

CASPER

Afraid—and for me, right?

MINA

What's happened between you? You wept, my friend?

CASPER

These tears; I will soon forget them if you wish. Mina, remember the gentle words that you said to me one day—love is a chaste and pure feeling that we can admit because it's God that has put it in our heart?

MINA

Yes, I said that and I remember.

CASPER

True love, you said, is the orphan's consolation, through it, the saddest past is forgotten—through it, the darkest future can yet be embellished.

MINA

Well—?

CASPER

Well, Mina—As for me, I'm an orphan, and God has sent me love to console me. My life until this day had been quite sad, and my future announces itself to be even sadder— But I love you, Mina, and the past can be forgotten and the future can be beautiful.

MINA

You love me?

CASPER

Yes, all the emotions that loves gives us, I experience in hearing you speak. Oh, you spoke truly; love makes us forget and consoles us—because, since you are here, since your hand is in mine—it seems to me I am less wretched. Mina, I forget, and I hope—you love me, too. These cares that you ceaselessly lavish on me, this tender affection with which you surround me—all this—this—

MINA

All that, Casper, is friendship.

CASPER

Friendship!

MINA

Oh, yes! A very tender friendship. A lively compassion for all your sufferings. That's all I experience.

CASPER

Great God!

MINA

But my love—

CASPER

Well?

MINA

My love is for someone else.

CASPER

And this someone else, this someone else?

MINA

It's Frederic.

CASPER

(weeping)

Frederic—Frederic.

MINA

He loved me before saving you, and I love him more—I do—for what he's done for you.

CASPER

(low)

So there's nothing more, nothing more in this world for poor Casper. Neither the friendship of Schwartz, nor my mother's, nor his love for her! My God, what do you want me to do on this earth, since the family you've given me is being torn from me? Since the one I've wanted to make rejects me?

(Enter Frederic)

FREDERIC

Receive my goodbyes, Mina. I'm leaving immediately with Casper. We no longer have anything to fear for him—he's entrusted to me.

CASPER

(calmly)

Frederic, my brother, no—you shall not leave, this order by the Count will not be carried our. You will remain by the one you love and who loves you, too. You will stay because it's not necessary that we all be wretched.

FREDERIC

What are you saying? Why he will refuse?

CASPER

No, you shall stay. I promise you. Your marriage will soon be accomplished. Let her be happy, friend, let her be happy.

COUNT

(entering with Baroness)

The Councilors that the Court of Vienna is sending and who precede the Baron have arrived at the castle. These men are the judges of your mother, mine. They are going to question you.

CASPER

Let 'em come, sir. And fear nothing from Casper. But first (in a whisper to the Baroness) Mother, once more—kiss your son.

BARONESS

Oh!

CASPER

Now, Casper has no more mother, no family; Casper is alone in the world. Let them question him. His response is prepared.

(At a sign from the Count the Councilors are introduced.)

A COUNCILOR

Herr Count, we've already been told, this young man is the one that you have sheltered, and whose birth is engulfed in a strange mystery. The Emperor has appointed us to help the Baron in the investigation he must make to discover Casper's persecutors.

CASPER

The investigation will be useless.

ALL

What do you mean?

CASPER

My persecutors no longer exist. God has called them to him. And as for me, I've forgiven them. The secret of my birth which they unveiled to me, and that I alone know—I intend to take with me to the tomb—on the day of my death.

(General astonishment. Casper goes to the Count and extend his hand to him.)

COUNT

(shaking his hand)

Casper! Casper!

CASPER

Now you no longer want to die, right?

(he pulls the ring from him)

COUNT

What are you doing? That ring—

CASPER

Tell the Emperor that the will I've just expressed here must be holy and sacred to all, because this will is that of a dying man.

(Casper puts the ring to his mouth)

COUNT

Heavens! He's lost! The poison—

ALL

Poison!

(They surround Casper)

BARONESS

Casper, my ch—

CASPER

(shutting her mouth)

Silence! I cannot live without causing ruin. I'm dying to save you. Pray for Casper. He's going to join Schwartz.

CURTAIN

ABOUT THE TRANSLATOR

Frank J. Morlock has written and translated many plays since retiring from the legal profession in 1992. His translations have also appeared on Project Gutenberg, the Alexandre Dumas Père web page, Literature in the Age of Napoléon, Infinite Artistries.com, and Munsey's (formerly Blackmask). In 2006 he received an award from the North American Jules Verne Society for his translations of Verne's plays. He lives and works in México.

www.ingramcontent.com/pod-product-compliance
Lightning Source LLC
LaVergne TN
LVHW041626070426
835507LV00008B/481